OVERCOMING CANCER

with God

Finding Peace and Hope in the Face of Adversity

PAMELA MALINCHAK

Copy Editor Donna Ferrier
Cover and Interior Design by Teagarden Designs

ISBN: 978-0-578-68269-3—paperback
        978-0-9818377-0-3—ebook

This book is dedicated to my Lord and Savior Jesus Christ, and to my dear and loving God.

Special thanks to my loving husband, William Malinchak, for his faithfulness to God and me.

To our children, Courtney, Taylor, Ashley, and Michael for bringing us true joy and love.

To my Mom and Dad, Anne and Anton Duswalt, for being the best parents ever!

To my brother, Craig; his wife, Natasha; and Tyler, Ryan, and Hayden for your love and support.

Contents

Introduction

One moment can drastically change our lives—one word, one accident, or one diagnosis. I heard the three words that changed my life on September 26, 2018: "You have cancer."

I don't think I ever imagined I would be diagnosed with cancer, but somehow it became real on that day. In that moment, my life *felt* different, and it *was* different. My sense of normalcy was continuing to evolve. Most people who have cancer say, "I'm battling cancer," and I agree it *is* a battle, but I chose to *surrender* that battle to God. I chose to live out God's greater story of my life. We are made in the image of God and we are designed to live on earth for His purposes. So how could I ask Him "Why me?"

When I stopped to think about everything, I realized that God's plan for my life was perfect. Before my diagnosis, I spent many hours getting to *know* God more than I ever had before. Up to that point, I usually read the Bible a few minutes a day, but a year before my diagnosis, my life was consumed with reading the Bible for sometimes up to eight hours per day. I would read God's Word and then listen to Daily Hope. Then after lunch, I would read God's Word some more and listen to Christian music.

After reading many books, I was inspired to keep a gratitude journal in which I wrote down everything I am thankful for. First on my list was *God*; anything else

I was grateful for continued from there. Keeping this journal also allowed me to write down Bible verses, important quotes from books, and any information that would help me become a better version of myself. Reading God's Word and applying it to my life was extremely helpful and it brought me great joy. As I continued to read the Bible, the Holy Spirit opened my heart to receive Godly wisdom, which brought comfort and healing.

When I was diagnosed with Stage 3 Rectal Cancer, I knew God had prepared me for this. I trusted He would be with me throughout this journey. God did not promise us an easy life. Jesus says in John 16:33, "I have said these things to you, that in me you may have peace. In the world you will have tribulation. But take heart; I have overcome the world." So, I never asked, "Why?" because I already knew the answer. God had *renewed* my mind. Was I going to let this circumstance change my belief in God's plan for my life?

We are not exempt from the trials of this life. In fact, Jesus asked, "How? How might my Father be glorified through this trial?" God uses trials like cancer, addiction, and death to bring us closer to Him. My cancer journey allowed me to depend on Him to get through the daily tasks of treatment. In John 9:3, "... his disciples asked him, 'Rabbi, who sinned, this man or his parents, that he was born blind?' Jesus answered, 'It was not that this man sinned, or his parents, but that the works of God might be displayed in him.'"

Our faith can be shaken when we go through difficult circumstances *if* we don't trust in our heavenly Father. God is always faithful, and He is unchangeable. Sometimes our views of God can change if what we were praying for didn't happen the way we wanted or the time we wanted, and we may *blame* God because we cannot see God's plan for our lives. We must have faith in God, therefore, and *not* in our circumstances. God is always good even when those *bad* things happen to us.

I grew up believing all things will work out for good, according to God's purpose. Looking back on my 56 years on this planet, my attitude isn't surprising because when I was growing up, most things *were* good! I was raised in the bucolic town of Deer Park, New York, with an older brother, Craig, and two loving parents who are still alive and married today. Though we came from a modest background, we didn't consider ourselves poor, and we never desired the great luxuries of life— primarily because we'd never seen or experienced them. Life may not have been perfect, but it was good.

We attended a small Episcopal church on Sundays, in which we experienced wonderful worship and fellowship. Despite breaking my front tooth on the church floor, I loved attending services and being part of a community, perhaps because of the donuts we ate after each service in the fellowship hall. Whatever the case, my parents were very involved in our church. They were Sunday School teachers and organized and participated in plays.

While I loved Sundays with my family, I didn't grow up having a deep and personal relationship with God. I believed in God and knew about Jesus, but I wasn't a true Christian. The only time I read the Bible was aloud in Sunday school.

I was relatively healthy as a child. I had mono at age 16 and a few bouts with bronchitis and pneumonia, and that was about it as far as any kind of serious illness was concerned. I attended a large public high school on Long Island, and I loved every day of school—maybe not the academics (which I regret to this day) but the social part. I had been a cheerleader since I was five. And since I had an older brother, I enjoyed playing all kinds of sports with his friends: baseball, softball, football, and basketball. I also loved gymnastics and performing in dance recitals.

After junior high, I turned to dance and cheerleading full time. I had a great relationship with all my friends on both those teams, and they were fun!

After high school, I began modeling and attended a college that was close to home. If you had seen me as a young girl, you would have never thought I would select a career as a model. But somehow it just happened, and despite all the years of not feeling pretty, I became a model.

A few years after my modeling career began, I was introduced to my wonderful husband, William. He had a quiet confidence and loved God! On our first date, we had such an intimate conversation about God and our beliefs. It was not my typical first date with someone, but it was so *real*. We formed a beautiful relationship, and we were engaged and married in less than nine months!

William was also raised from humble beginnings in Monessen, Pennsylvania. Working from the time he was eight years old, William delivered the newspaper. Always a very active and athletic young boy, he participated in all sports but fell in love with football. In fact, he had an inner yearning to make it to the NFL, so from an early age, he started reading *The Power of Positive Thinking* by Norman Vincent Peale and making tape recordings to listen to every night before he went to bed. His tenacity and belief in God and himself paved the way for his dream to come true, and he had a ten-year career as a wide receiver with the Detroit Lions and the Washington Redskins.

From the moment we met, our Lord has been the foundation of our relationship. We have continually prayed together and worked through difficult situations with God's help. We are truly grateful for God and His mercy. I'm not sure how anyone can go through this life alone, especially in the face of a life-threatening diagnosis like cancer.

We had been regularly attending church from the moment we met, and it has always felt like home to us. We value our relationships with our church family. We seek real fellowship with one another and experience life together. We are called to belong, not just to believe. Ephesians 2:20-21 says "Together, we are his house, built on the foundation of the apostles and the prophets.

And the cornerstone is Christ Jesus himself. We are carefully joined together in him, becoming a holy temple for the Lord."

William is definitely the spiritual leader of our family. He has a beautiful relationship with God and never misses reading his Bible daily. He spends hours reading and writing a true love letter to God in his daily journal. It's amazing and so wonderful to watch my husband love God with his entire being and giving thanks and glory to Him every day. I believe he has read the Bible from beginning to end at least fifteen times. He makes me want to read more and do more for God. He truly inspires me, and I feel so blessed to have him as my husband.

We have also been blessed with four wonderful children! It's amazing how much I discovered I could love once I had kids. We raised them the best way we could. Sometimes we sailed through smoothly, while other times were more challenging. We were not perfect parents, but we have always loved our children and prayed to God, the perfect parent, for them daily. We raised them in full partnership with God, who always provided protection for them beyond anything we could give. We know He didn't promise our family would be perfect, but praying for them released the power of God to work in their lives. So, we had the peace of God as we enjoyed the process of watching our children grow and develop.

I chose to be a stay-at-home mom throughout most of their lives, but I received a great opportunity to work at the Christian school our children attended and began working as a teaching assistant when our youngest child was in the eighth grade. This allowed me to see them during the day and have their friends visit me in my classroom, as well. Being a mom has been the greatest gift and blessing! I am truly grateful for being able to carry and care for our children throughout their lives. It truly is a special love that continues to grow.

William and I are now empty nesters! Our home is so quiet, and we miss all the talking and busyness our lives once had. We miss driving the kids to school, to their daily practices, and weekends filled with games and tournaments. William was our son Michael's baseball coach. He spent most of his time at practices and games with him while I was with our girls through years of gymnastics, then tennis, and finally golf. Now, they're young adults pursuing their dreams in different areas of the United States.

Once the last of our children left the house, William and I started learning to be alone again and sharing quality time with each other. It's amazing that although we had spent so much time together raising our children, we almost got reacquainted with one another once our children left home. Life was different, but we were learning to enjoy our time together and think about *ourselves* for once.

I took a year off from my teaching assistant job and then returned to work once again. About a week before the start of the school year, my mother called to inform me that my dad had fallen again. Unfortunately, it had happened a few times, but this was a bad fall that resulted in a hospital stay with six broken ribs, a punctured lung, and cuts and bruises. William and I knew they both needed to come to Florida so we could take care of them.

My parents arrived in Florida at the beginning of September that year. A few days later, I woke up one morning and felt a small lump that suddenly protruded from my left groin. Women always seem to notice anything new that suddenly appears on our bodies, and this little bump wasn't there the night before. I felt it and even tried to push it back in, but that didn't work. I showed the lump to William and we decided to see my gynecologist, who I have known for twenty-seven years. He felt we should give it a week to see if it was still there. But the following week, the swelling was the same, so he told me to see a vascular surgeon. We met with the surgeon the next day, but he was unable to do a biopsy because he was unsure if the lump was a hernia or lymph node.

So my doctor decided to do exploratory surgery—on September 20, 2018, *our anniversary*. I was supposed to be taking care of my parents, but instead they were sitting with William in the hospital waiting room—waiting for me! While this was obviously not what I expected, that's the wonderful part about our journey: God has planned the days of our lives in advance, and this was for His purpose. Nothing in our lives is arbitrary.

The surgery went according to plan and I was feeling good. My doctor informed us that it was a lymph node that had gone awry and that he was sending the report to a pathologist. We were all optimistic because our doctor felt everything looked good. I'd had four c-sections, but now I had a small scar going in the opposite direction of my c-section scars.

Then, the unexpected phone call came! My surgeon sounded a bit concerned and almost surprised by the pathologist's findings. I had *CANCER*—squamous cell carcinoma. I was surprised to say the least, but somehow took the news fairly well. I never expected my doctor to say the word *cancer,* referring to me, but we all go through trials whether it be sickness, loneliness, addiction, depression, or death. Usually we wonder, *Why does life have to be so difficult?* From reading the Bible the answer is because "sin" entered this world. But the good news is our Savior Jesus Christ died for our sins, so we can be with our Lord forever.

While that phone call definitely changed our lives, it would be for the better! I would grow to have a deeper intimacy with God and a more beautiful relationship with William and my family and friends.

When I hung up the phone and walked into William's office, I shared the news with him. He was a bit surprised to say the least, but as William always does, he said a beautiful prayer for me that covered me in God's arms. We knew everything was going to be good because we trusted in God's plan for us.

Do you believe that God may allow situations to *appear* just to show you that Jesus is the only stable one in your life and that He will bring you peace and comfort? That's why He is called *the Prince of Peace.* The Bible says, "Call upon me in the day of trouble; I will deliver you, and you shall Glorify me"(Psalm 50:15). When you depend on God, it honors Him.

We scheduled a meeting with an oncologist in Florida to figure out my next steps. That's when all the tests began—PET scans, MRIs, CAT scans, bloodwork, you name it. After trying to figure out the source of the cancer, my rectal doctor discovered the tumor. He immediately knew it was rectal cancer even while he was performing the biopsy. A few days later, when he called to confirm that it was indeed rectal cancer, he also told me the treatment would be chemotherapy and radiation. Again, somehow I took the news well. That was God! He was with me every step of the way...every day...every hour...every minute...every second. Thank you, God!

God also provides. Seven years ago, my mother was having her hair colored and another woman sitting next to her was listening to the conversation that my mom was sharing with her hairdresser. She was explaining that my aunt was in the hospital, suffering from cancer. This woman slipped my mom a piece of loose-leaf paper with the name of her brother-in-law, who was an oncologist at Sloan Kettering, the premier cancer treatment hospital in New York City. My mom thanked her and put the paper in her pocketbook.

Unfortunately, she was unable to share that information with my aunt because she passed away shortly after this conversation.

When I shared with my mom the news of my cancer diagnosis (which was seven years after my mom's conversation at her hairdresser), she asked me where I was going to be treated, and my answer was "Sloan Kettering." My mom was crying because she told me that while she was cleaning out her pocketbook, she found this piece of paper with the name of a colorectal oncologist at Sloan Kettering. She'd kept that piece of paper all this time. God knew I would be diagnosed with rectal cancer and He had already appointed that specific doctor to treat me at that particular hospital.

I know that God loves us and is always there to help. He sent His son to give us hope and a future. Our hope is in Jesus, even when we feel something happens in our lives that we don't expect or when our lives don't play out like we think they should. God's plans are bigger than ours. So celebrate the gift of grace that was revealed in Jesus' death for our sins. Hold on to faith in Him.

*"For I know the plans I have
for you," says the Lord.
"They are plans for good
and not for disaster, to give
you a future and a hope."*

—Jeremiah 29:11 (NLT)

One Day at a Time

As I lay in bed, my mind started racing. William and I knew we had made the right decision to go to Sloan Kettering. And since my mom had shared the story with me about the colorectal oncologist at Sloan, I knew the decision was God's leading, and I had to follow Him.

It was still a difficult decision because we had to leave the comfort of our beautiful home in Florida and spend two months in a hotel in New York, which was also going to be extremely expensive. Plus, I was not used to the cold temperatures in New York and we would be leaving mid-October. But William and I believed going to Sloan was the right decision, so we left our home, hopped on a plane, and never looked back.

When we arrived in New York, we chose to stay in a hotel close to the hospital since I was scheduled to receive daily treatments. My first appointments were in the outpatient pavilion on 53rd Street. My radiation treatments would be in a different location at the hospital on 68th Street.

William and I arrived at the hospital at eight in the morning and walked into the outpatient pavilion; it was so surreal. I felt completely healthy with no signs of pain, so I started to wonder, *Do I really have cancer? Do I really have to take chemo and radiation?* But somehow I continued on. After I signed in, I had to fill out tons of paperwork. Thankfully I brought all of my medical records from Florida, which showed the tests my doctors had done, and my diagnosis.

A few minutes later, a nurse brought me into a room with other patients to take my vitals, draw some blood, and weigh me. Afterward I went back to the oversized waiting room to sit with William; my parents; and our daughter, Taylor. I was very grateful that Taylor and my parents could spend the day with us while we met with my team of doctors. Taylor often worries about her mom, and my parents had to travel from Long Island to be there—they've always supported me.

All of us gathered in the exam room to meet with my medical oncologist. First we were introduced by a nurse, then a fellow, and finally my doctor. They discussed my situation and the treatment plan for me, which I already knew was going to be chemo and radiation. I would receive six weeks of daily treatments, Monday through Friday, totaling twenty-seven days of chemo and radiation.

My family and I listened to the doctor communicate the medications I would be taking and the side effects, though I tried to blur out the part about the side effects. While I appreciated the extensive experience and knowledge of the medical professionals regarding the latest developments in cancer treatments and technologies, I was happy when the conversations were finally over because I didn't want to think about my treatments.

After this appointment, we left the doctor's office and ate some sandwiches that William had brought us from a nearby deli. After lunch, I met with the rectal oncologist and she performed a rectal exam, which was a bit uncomfortable. Then she discussed the results of the exam and the method of radiation she would be using to get rid of the tumor.

We then left her office and met with a gynecologist oncologist to discuss other findings and to have an MRI. The doctor injected contrast in my IV for the MRI and gave me some cookies and apple juice to eat once the test was finished. An hour or so later, I was feeling quite nauseous and believed it was a prelude to my chemo treatments.

The following day, I had an appointment with my radiation oncologist to discuss how the radiation treatments would be done. He told us it would take at least a week to meet with some physicists to figure out my particular treatment. I didn't ask too many questions about my exact treatment because I knew it would be my only option and I didn't want to hear anything else. The doctor discussed the side effects, and although I was a bit scared, I remained positive.

William and I tried to enjoy Manhattan as much as we could while we were there before I began my chemo and radiation treatments, but I was just going through the motions. I pretended I was happy, but I didn't feel happy because I knew I was about to endure the toughest fight of my life. That's why it was important for me to stay positive and not let any negative thoughts enter my mind.

The next day, the radiation oncologist made an appointment for me to be "fitted" for my treatments. The nurse administered an IV in my arm and gave me a "mixture" to drink so I could be fitted for a mold. Then the radiation team poured a warm mold, which formed around my body, from my waist to my mid thighs, and became a cast. Next, my team did what they called a "simulation," which is a practice run without giving radiation therapy.

Then they used the imaging scans to identify the tumor location and put four tiny tattoos on my body so that every day they knew where to target the radiation. The doctor inserted one tiny needle in my pubic area, one a little lower than my belly button and one on each side of my hips.

Day after day, as I continued to go through scans and tests, the whole process was becoming more and more real to William and me. We both tried to stay positive, and I kept smiling through all the tests and trials life was throwing at me. It was a choice I made and continue to make daily.

Do you find you're closer to God when you are facing a difficult time in your life? Why can't we feel close to God or feel the desire to spend time in His word when things are not going well? I knew that clinging to God was the only way I was going to get through this. I needed hope. Hope is expecting that we will know God in all circumstances, even the difficult ones.

Should we not have hope and trust in such a mighty God? I prayed, "God, I know this cancer diagnosis is an opportunity for me and my family. I know this adventure is scary and I am putting my faith and trust in you. I know you have a plan for my life and to help others have an opportunity to know you better. Help me to share your love for your glory." Our future is secure in Jesus Christ. He freely offers His gift of eternal life for our sins, but we need to reach out to Him and ask for that forgiveness.

"I have told you all this so that you may have peace in me. Here on earth you will have many trials and sorrows. But take heart, because I have overcome the world."

—John 16:33

Day One

It was a Friday morning and my appointment for bloodwork was scheduled at eight. William and I woke up early to get ready for this life-changing day. I was about to begin treatments for cancer.

How those words don't seem real. But today, William and I have the peace and comfort of God, who walked with me during this trial. I put my trust in Him. You may wonder, *How can you trust God when life seems so difficult?* God never promised us a perfect life here on earth. We need to remember the story in Genesis of mankind's fall, which caused us to rebel against God and caused the once-perfect physical bodies God had given us to experience sickness and death.

The Good News is that our Lord does not leave us in the midst of the mess that we brought into the world. He sent His only Son, Jesus, to reunite us with God and each other. When we put our faith in God and believe in Him, He gives us the hope we need to face the difficulties in life. God will never abandon you.

When we entered the hospital, the receptionist checked me in and asked us to be seated. In the waiting room were my parents, who had just arrived from Long Island. It was wonderful to have them spend the day with us.

Immediately a receptionist called my name and brought me to a private room where a nurse collected my basic health information...weight, height, vitals, and blood pressure. Then she drew some blood from the back of my hand. I didn't know the reason at the time, but discovered it later on.

After the bloodwork, my family and I met with my medical oncologist. After reviewing my bloodwork and vitals, he felt I was healthy enough to get my Chemo IV that day.

We all proceeded to follow through the double doors with the words "Chemo Area" printed above them, on the wall. There must have been at least 15 rooms available for patients to receive chemotherapy. I had been really scared the entire morning, but I was unable to talk about it. I was just ready to get it done.

I looked at William and I could sense his concern. He was probably wondering *How did this all happen? Is my wife really about to receive chemo?* We smiled at each other and shook our heads because we silently knew it would all be good.

My nurse was extremely gentle and explained everything that was going to happen. First, she put an IV in my vein and then added some saline to make sure it was in properly. Then she put on her scrubs, mask, and gloves. I was thinking, *Now, it's getting pretty serious*! She asked me, "How are you doing?"

I told her, "I'm good!" In reality, I was so nervous when she finally inserted the chemo into my IV. I felt this cold sensation running through my body. I became numb and I just wanted to leave, but I knew I had to face this new reality. William and I had been praying all morning, but at this point I knew I just had to trust God that everything was going to be good.

My mom and dad tried to lighten the mood by sharing funny stories to make me laugh. Although this helped me feel some peace, I was still feeling a bit anxious. All I could do was silently pray.

Finally, it was over! William and I just sat there for a moment before walking out of the room. I didn't feel different or nauseous or anything, *yet.*

William ordered some lunch for all of us, which we ate as we left on a shuttle bus to travel to a different location for my radiation treatment. When we arrived, we took the elevator to the fourth floor where I checked in and met my medical team.

William, my parents, and I sat in the waiting room where there were many others waiting to be treated. I was becoming more anxious because I didn't know how the treatment would feel. Suddenly, the receptionist called my name, and I left William and my parents to go into a dressing room *alone.* As I entered the dressing room, I quietly asked God to bring me some peace. I needed to feel His presence at that moment. Oh, how I was so scared! But I found a hospital gown that was neatly folded in the cabinets, slowly undressed, and put it on.

As I walked through another doorway, I was greeted by one of my radiation therapists, who walked me through the radiation department and bought me to my treatment room. I was also greeted by two women who were also part of my radiation team. The radiation machines were huge! The therapist asked me to lay down on the table inside my cast. Once I laid down, the team slid a blanket underneath me to position me carefully in a frog-like position. I was then handed a dilator to insert into my vagina to prevent the radiation from shutting the walls down since the radiation would be targeting the lymph node in my pelvic area and in my rectal area.

Finally, I was all set when suddenly they told me they were going to leave. *I was going to be all alone!* Instantly, I became anxious, so I chose to pray Philippians 4:6 "Do not be anxious about anything, but everything by prayer and supplication with thanksgiving let your requests be made known to God." I knew I needed to have more faith. Anxiety changes us and it changes our perception. We know there is no logical explanation for worrying, but somehow we *all* do it. There is a battlefield in our minds, and we need to go to Christ. We have to learn to "be still" and rest in God's presence. I knew I had to acknowledge *who* God is and relax, breathe, and trust in Him.

The enormous machine began to move and started circling around me. Not long after it came to a halt, I heard a buzzing and beeping noise that lasted about 20 seconds. This cycle repeated over and over to give me the radiation treatment. It was not something I enjoyed, so I wanted to take my mind off it all! Oh, how I wanted it to stop!

A small paint chip on the ceiling in front of me became my focus as I prayed "I can do all things through Christ who strengthens me" over and over the entire time I was receiving radiation. It seemed like it was never going to end, so I just kept on praying as the machine just kept on buzzing. Then, after 20–30 minutes, it all stopped, finally! Next the automatic door opened slowly and the radiation team came in with all smiles, saying, "We're done!" I was truly happy!

One woman escorted me back to the dressing room. Afterward, I washed up in the bathroom and proceeded to get dressed. I was truly grateful for it to be over and see William and my parents! They gave me some wonderful hugs! They asked me how the treatment went. It was easier not to talk about my treatment and all I had to endure, so I simply said, "Good."

We walked home from the hospital because it was only 5 blocks from our hotel. I felt I was being a little quiet, but my mind was racing about everything. I wanted to stop it all and go home, but I couldn't. I had to deal with this right then. God can heal the brokenhearted and fill that emptiness with His love. Life is always easier when I completely trust God because I have peace since God is bigger than any problem. Nothing else compares to what God can offer us—eternal and blissful peace. So I trust God because He is on my team.

I was so grateful to get back to our hotel, the Bristol Plaza on East 65th Street. This was a beautiful, extended-stay hotel, which also had a discounted rate for patients from Sloan Kettering.

William and I enjoyed this one-bedroom, which included a kitchen where I could make my meals, and a living room. The kitchen was very small, but that didn't matter because it had a stove and a refrigerator, and that was all I needed to make me happy.

Since I was feeling well that night, I made dinner for all of us. After dinner, I took my chemo pills for the first time. Every morning I took five and in the evenings I took four. For the record, I don't like taking any pills.

My parents decided to stay the evening, so they slept on the pull-out couch in our living room. We didn't discuss anything about my treatment, but I could sense they were concerned. They wanted to share memories with us, whether or not they were good memories. I feel blessed to be their daughter and I am grateful for them.

Although this life-changing event had me rattled, I believed God wouldn't have allowed this to happen unless He had a plan. So I trusted God for His everlasting mercy and goodness.

"When I am afraid, I put my trust in you."

—*Psalm 56:3 (NLT)*

Weekends

It was Saturday, which meant no radiation or chemo! Even though I had just begun treatment, having been poked and prodded with many tests and scans, it was nice to take a day off. So we stayed in and just talked, trying to get our minds off everything.

My parents decided to leave later that afternoon. I think they thought I was fine, so they probably wanted to go home and sleep in their comfortable bed instead of the pull-out sofa.

After dinner, I started to feel pretty nauseous, similar to when I was pregnant with our children. So William and I went to bed early that evening and then during the night I felt even worse.

I spent so much time in the bathroom because I was having bouts of diarrhea all night. After each trip to the bathroom, I would climb back into bed and just lie there feeling sick.

When I woke up Sunday morning, I was so nauseous I couldn't get out of bed. After a few hours, I asked myself, "How am I going to do this? Am I going to feel like this every day? I'm not too sure I can handle this." So I did the only thing I knew how to do: I humbly asked God to get me through this. The answer He gave me was "One day at a time."

That began my mindset. I didn't think of tomorrow, just today. I thought of how I could make myself feel better *now*. At first, William suggested trying to eat some saltine crackers because that's what helped me through my pregnancies. So I ate some and it helped a little, though I still felt nauseous. From that moment, I chose to eat, even when my stomach and body said "No!" I knew that eating would restore me and make me feel healthy.

For breakfast, I decided to make scrambled eggs, and I had to force them down. The nurse suggested I take an anti-nausea pill. I tried it, but I still felt nauseous.

Our children called to see how I was feeling, and I tried to remain positive and said I was doing well. I could sense their concern. I'm sure William shared with them exactly what was happening.

Throughout each day, I would nibble on crackers and take a teaspoon of ginger ale. William was very concerned and wanted to help. Oh, how grateful I am for him! It must have been really difficult for him to watch his wife suffer through the pain, the hospital visits, the traveling, the worrying, the grocery shopping, and the praying. I'm sure he could have been doing something else, but he came to every appointment with me and never left my side! I'm sure there were moments he felt helpless and uncomfortable, but he never turned away. Instead he continued to try to help me feel better.

William and I prayed together all day. I knew not to welcome the *What-if* thoughts. *What if I feel like this all the time? What if I never get better?* I knew I didn't have control over myself, so I chose to surrender to God and ask Him to take control of my life. I fully surrendered to Him. I depended on God's strength to get me through it. We need to take all our fears and the *What ifs* to God and ask Him to take over. It seemed like we asked God every hour of the day to help me get through this. And He did!

"Worship the Lord your God, and his blessing will be on your food and water. I will take away sickness from among you."

—Exodus 23:25 (NIV)

Day Two

Monday morning! William and I usually woke up early, but this day *was* different because I was not feeling well, so I was awake most of the night. But during that sleepless night, Christ remained constant and He is sufficient. He stayed close to me and kept me safe. I had already accepted God's plan for me, and as I continued to surrender to Him, William and I wanted to worship God more.

When I want to read about surrender, I always look to Abraham in the book of Genesis. God wanted Him to leave his country and his family to lead a nation. Humbly Abraham continued to trust and obey God even when He asked Abraham to offer his son, Isaac, as a burnt offering. He understood that worshipping God was greater than any gift he had received from Him, so he chose to let go. Thankfully, however, Abraham didn't have to go through with the sacrifice of his only son. In reading Abraham's story, I have also learned to let go and let God.

The Bible tells us that we have now become new creations in Christ. Our slates have been wiped clean, and now we have a new beginning, when we are willing to work with the Lord and trust in Him. As you surrender your life to God the Father, He will lead you to His perfect plan over your life.

What are you holding on to?

I am learning to let go of my control. For a long time, I wanted to control almost everything with my family. I wanted to make sure they were always healthy and safe. In other words, my control was rooted in fear. Over the years, I have learned to replace fear with faith. Many of us have fears but practicing the truth that "God is with me" can lessen those fears. When you become more aware that God is near, somehow you lose your fear. The Bible says, "There is no fear in love. But perfect love casts out all fear" (1 John 4:18) . When you feel the love of God, fear disappears. There is something in all of us that is hard to let go, but God is encouraging William and me to trust Him.

When we arrived at the hospital, a nurse called my name and I walked into the women's dressing room. She asked me to undress from the waist down. While in the dressing room, I was praying for peace and comfort. I said to God, "Oh heavenly Father, I am nervous, and I need your strength to get me through this day. You are faithful. You are worthy of my trust and I put my confidence in you. Please take all my fears and anxiety away and bring me your peace. Thank you for your love for me, and I am truly grateful. I love you!"

When I face trials, God is my comforter. He is always there for me when I feel alone, so I tell Him how I feel. I tell Him when I am scared, lonely, sad, or tired. This is a significant part of the relationship I have with God. God wants me to be in a relationship with Him, just like I'm in a relationship with my parents, spouse, and friends. You may be feeling lonely or sad or receiving a diagnosis of cancer. How do you get through it? I know that running away from God is not the answer but running towards Him will bring you peace and comfort. God has a plan for our lives and He will never leave us. It's about fulfilling God's desire to know Him more every day.

Remember the Apostle Paul said we have peace *with* God. That word *with* makes quite a difference. Paul didn't say we have "peace of God" or "God's peace in us" which are both true. The way Paul describes this kind of peace, is a spiritual peace with His family. Jesus made this possible because He wanted to- enough to suffer and die on the cross for us. How amazing is that? What a Savior!

Slowly I slipped into my hospital gown with the opening to the back. As I entered the radiation room, I proceeded to take my boots off while leaving my socks on to keep me warm. Gingerly, I lay onto the table and fit myself into the mold. Again, I inserted the dilator and endured another 30 minutes of radiation front and behind with the treatment team closely monitoring me. Every time the radiation machine stopped at a different angle, I heard that buzzing sound. As I was going through it, once again I found that little white spot on the wall where I continually prayed, "I can do all things through Christ who strengthens me." My mind drifted off sometimes, but I tried to remain positive. When the doors finally opened, I could hear the angels sing... well not really, but that's how I felt. I wanted to sing "Alleluia!" right along with them.

When William and I returned to our hotel, we both got undressed and I took another shower before I applied more lotion in the areas where I had received the radiation.

After dinner, I proceeded to take another anti-nausea pill and then a few hours later my chemo pills. My doctor had suggested I take the chemo pills 12 hours apart, and encouraged me to drink a lot of water with them. So I tried to time them exactly 12 hours apart, but drinking the water was difficult because my stomach was always upset. So William would leave crackers and ginger ale on the nightstand next to me. And we would pray some more.

Guess what? I got through another day! Why? Because God got me through it...no other reason.

"When you go through deep waters, I will be with you."

—Isaiah 43:2 (NLT)

Day Three

Happy Tuesday! I woke up to my alarm, which was always set at 7:45. William was already up doing his morning exercises and reading the Bible. I looked around at our small hotel room and wished we could be in our own house. How I missed my home while I was receiving treatment. Everything I looked at made me miss Florida. I missed being able to sit at my desk and write on my computer about scripture and in my gratitude journal, praising God. I missed all of my alone time with Him. My head was just not in the right mindset, and it was difficult for me to focus and get back on track.

My stomach felt a little better, but I still took an anti-nausea pill before breakfast and then those chemo pills.

Every Tuesday, I meet with my radiation oncologist and his nurse for a quick checkup of my rectal area. They asked me lots of questions about my symptoms and then continued my usual radiation. They always did an extra scan or two on Tuesdays, but I always looked at the only white spot in the room and prayed "I can do all things through Christ who strengthens me." Jesus suffered on the cross for our sins and I cannot imagine the pain He endured. My pain seems so minimal compared to His. That thought helped me get through my daily treatments. Finally, the doors opened and I was thrilled! I say my goodbyes and *hurried* out!

God saw me in my pain and suffering. He saw me when I was facing those difficult trials and my life was turned upside down. He saw me every time I cried out to Him in despair. Although my prayers were not answered immediately, God answered them all in His time. He sent His own son, Jesus, to provide for me; He wanted me to know and feel the hope found in Him.

By God's grace, He gave me eyes to see that I was not the only one suffering. William and I always enjoyed watching people come in with a friend or a loved one to offer them support, but I saw so many people waiting to be treated for cancer, and some of them were alone. That made my heart sad and God had already revealed to me that I would have true compassion for those people. As I walk this life, I often wonder about God's plan for me, but God always teaches me His goodness through my moments with friends, family, and people I meet daily. While I was experiencing this uncertainty with cancer, the faithfulness of other believers in Christ touched my heart. God uses people to share hugs, words, and acts of service to feel His presence. Without their love and support, my treatment would be much more difficult. God calls us to help and encourage those in the middle of a crisis. The miracle of encouragement is that God can use a kind word or a smile to emulate Christ for the person who is in pain.

On the advice of a friend, I started keeping a journal. It helped me keep track not only of my daily food intake, water, pills, and medicines, but also my thoughts, emotions, and people I meet every day. I realized

I needed to stay positive and to bring joy, love, and hope whenever I had the opportunity.

Some people blog about their experiences with cancer, as well. I chose not to share my diagnosis of the *type* of cancer with many people because I have learned that someone will want to share with you how their best friend or family member passed away with the same type of cancer. I know that some actresses have been diagnosed with my type of cancer and they eventually lost their battle to cancer. I kept to myself and some faithful friends and trusted in God to help me through this time. I tried to stay in the Word and to pray continuously.

As I was going through my treatments, I was reading *The Faith Walk: A Path Toward Holiness* that William purchased for me. It was a wonderful devotional for me. That day, the book shared that I am never alone and that God is accompanying me on this journey! "He is a faithful friend to the end." Oh, how I needed to read that at a time in my life when deep down I was struggling to believe that God would lead me to what is best for my life.

There was always a daily choice to make: Would I choose faith or fear? It was faith that drove me to move forward, but that didn't mean the fear went away completely. I had to choose to fight this fight of faith, when *faced with cancer.* I believed in the goodness of God and I knew I had a difficult journey ahead. I needed to keep my faith *alive.*

God may allow us to experience some fear because in the process it teaches us to trust Him. "We rejoice in our sufferings, knowing that suffering produces endurance, and endurance produces character, and character produces hope, and hope does not put us to shame, because God's love has been poured into our hearts through the Holy Spirit who has been given to us" (Romans 5:3-5). We have hope because of God's love who lives in our hearts by the Holy Spirit.

Reading and believing the truth will set you free. Trust that God will get you through any suffering. He can heal you and guide you to people who can help you. God calls us to encourage one another, especially in times of need.

"Don't be afraid, for I am with you. Don't be discouraged, for I am your God. I will strengthen you and help you. I will hold you up with my victorious right hand."

—Isaiah 41:10 (NLT)

Day Four

It was Wednesday! I was halfway through the week! Woke up during the night, ate my crackers, and drank my ginger ale.

In the morning, I just lay in bed and watched some feel-good TV shows, usually a game show or a sweet Hallmark movie. William was always there with me, either joining in to watch a movie or reading the Bible, and I'm sure saying extra prayers for me!

Can you believe I made mashed potatoes at 10:30 that morning? My stomach always felt better when it wasn't empty, so I was always throwing a cracker in my mouth and drinking a tiny bit of ginger ale. Nutrition was a big part of my journey with rectal cancer. In fact, we met with an oncologist nutritionist that day to discuss it. She explained the importance of avoiding extreme weight loss during treatment because it can decrease the body's ability to fight the cancer. So she advised eating a well-balanced diet, encouraging extra calories to provide protein, vitamins, and minerals, that would nourish my body without affecting the symptoms. As my treatments would become more challenging, she explained I would need to stay away from fruits, vegetables, oils, butter, and dairy, because of the way they would affect my body.

My radiation treatment was routine. As always I tried not to think about what was happening to my body and I just prayed for God's peace because

I trusted Him completely. He promised that when life gets too hard, He will carry us through. Each time I face a challenge or get knocked down I know that God will be with me to *fight* my battles.

Is anything too hard for God? Definitely not. He created the universe out of nothing. Many people become discouraged and full of doubt. Let's look at Abraham who was 100 years old and he laughed at God when He said that his wife Sarah at age 90 would become pregnant. The Lord said, "I will surely return to you about this time next year, and Sarah your wife shall have a son" (Genesis 18:11). As we trust in the Lord and continue to pray, He promises to answer our prayers. Sometimes we have to wait because waiting on His perfect timing for our life helps develop our character. God is more interested in our character than in our comfort.

That evening William and I read some devotionals together, and God told us to *be strong.* I am trying to be strong. Jesus experienced many hard times here on earth. The road to the cross was not an easy task, but He had to go through it. When life gets too hard, we need to look at Him instead of our situation. So we acknowledged that God is bigger than any problem *or treatment.* He is in control, and He is the solution. Having true faith in God is believing He can do anything. Once I knew that, I started to believe all the 6,000 promises in the Bible.

"Do not be conformed to this world, but be transformed by the renewal of your mind, that by testing you may discern what is the will of God, what is good and acceptable and perfect."

—Romans 12:2 (ESV)

Day Five

It was Thursday! Woke up early after feeling nauseous most of the night, but maybe it was because I didn't have a bowel movement. *I know...too much information.*

William was wonderful throughout my treatments! We spent all our time together and I appreciated the sacrifice he made as he stopped his life to travel with me to New York to support me during my treatments. The words *thank you* just don't seem to be enough.

I try to tell him as often as possible how grateful I am for him and how much I appreciate him. The same goes for my Father in heaven; I am to thank Him for everything, *even when I am faced with difficult times.* The apostle Paul said, "Give thanks in all circumstances, for this is God's will for you in Christ Jesus." Even if certain situations in my life never change, my attitude toward them can. This makes all the difference.

Troubles brings us closer to Jesus so we will depend more on Him. Therefore, if the pain or difficult moments in your life causes you to depend more on God, then we are to thank Him for it. 1Thessalonians 5:18 says, "Give thanks in all circumstances; for this is the will of God in Christ Jesus for you." This verse does not imply to give thanks for everything- like cancer, but to give thanks in every circumstance. We can give thanks to our God because His purpose for our lives is bigger than our pain or problem.

I began seeking fulfilment in Christ alone. I realized that His love for me rested in His character, not in my diagnosis. I am choosing to remain faithful and grateful for God.

Becoming a grateful person can help you overcome any situation you are facing. If you choose to make a list and write all that you are grateful for, you will find that you are blessed. We need to make those daily or weekly lists of what we are thankful for our family, friends, God, and whatever and whoever else you are thankful. So, when you go through a difficult time, that's when you need to be reminded of *all* that God has blessed you with.

My medical oncologist said I had a 50/50 chance of losing my hair, though at this point, I had not lost it yet. It would definitely get thinner, however. So in my infinite wisdom, I chose not to *brush* my hair, well, at least not from the root. I would hold my hair loosely and very lightly brush the ends. It was still too early to notice any changes in my hair, but either way, it was all good.

Radiation was radiation, but it was now causing me to urinate more often. My therapist explained it was because they were targeting my bladder area. Even still, he gave me a bladder test to make sure I didn't have a bladder infection and it came back negative. Again I was truly grateful!

There was a snowstorm that day in New York City, so William and I had to walk home! Thankfully I had purchased some rain boots for the snow, but it was still hard to navigate through it. We appreciated the warmer climate in Florida, but we were enjoying the cooler temperatures.

When the sun was shining in Florida and life was good, we sometimes didn't seek out God. But during these desperate times we need to have more meaningful prayers. We learned to cry out to our Savior to deliver us from our pain and suffering. It reminds us that everything we have is a gift from God. In 2 Corinthians 12:9, Jesus said, "My grace is sufficient for you, for my power is made in perfect weakness." When we understand how much we need Him, especially when we are weak and tired, then Jesus can bring us His strength. Jesus always comes at the right moment, just when we need Him.

"Trust in the Lord with all your heart, and do not lean on your own understanding, In all your ways acknowledge Him, and He will make straight your paths."

—*Proverbs 3:5-6 (NIV)*

Day Six

Happy Friday! Thank you, God, for bringing me to that day! God has brought me many blessings through my trials. It really felt good once I learned how to pray and thank God, even if all I could pray was, "God, I don't know what is going to happen today, but I will trust you." The beautiful miracle was knowing I was never alone because God loves me and has a plan for my life. So He can use even the most difficult days for good. That's when miracles happen.

Every person who comes to God *is* a child of God. Michael Tyler, who wrote the song, "Different," explains so beautifully how to handle difficult situations. He first asked, "Jesus, can you stop these things, the cancer, and the storms?" When nothing changed he then asked God, "Can you change me so that I can handle these things?" I loved hearing that. As much as I wanted my circumstances to change when I faced a tough diagnosis, instead I looked to God to change me. God is my Father and He knows what is best for me.

How wonderful it was to hear from a friend or loved one that they cared and were thinking about me. It was so nice when people reached out and told me they were praying for me. My mental state drastically affected my recovery. When I was calm and peaceful, I was focusing on my body and trying to recover. A get-well card brightened my day and I will continue to send cards to others who need encouragement.

The weather was in the 30s that day—*quite chilly*! William and I enjoyed seeing everyone at the hospital because they were so friendly. As I noticed many people waiting to be treated, I began to realize how many people were going through the same process I was. All of us glanced at one another and offered a smile, but I could sense pain hidden behind those smiles.

That day, I met an adorable little girl being held by her mother as we were riding together in the elevator. She looked sad and I just smiled at her and told her I understood how she felt. She said, "You have the same treatment?"

Honestly, I wasn't too sure what her treatment was, but I felt safe enough to say "yes," since I was receiving both chemo and radiation. She gave me the cutest smile!

Her mother smiled at me and quietly whispered, "Thank you."

These were the days I felt truly happy to be part of this journey. I loved being there to help someone when they were not feeling well. I had experienced the pain, the hurt, and the fear and knew exactly what other people in the hospital were facing. It's difficult to empathize with someone when we don't know, from experience, how the other person is feeling. I believe when we experience difficult times, God comforts us and then we pass it on to others in need. "If we are afflicted, it is for your comfort and salvation; and if we are comforted, it is for your comfort, which you experience when you patiently endure the same sufferings that we suffer" (2 Corinthians 1:6).

When you are experiencing pain or suffering in your life, you don't look for someone who has done research on that particular area, you look for someone who has experienced the same type of pain. Our suffering can help others who are going through difficult moments.

I am equipped *now* to help someone who has been diagnosed with cancer. I can share the lessons I learned while going through the process. Suffering teaches us to depend on God. The Apostle Paul experienced much suffering, and when he looked back, he noticed a spiritual benefit. You can have peace because we know that God is always with us and He loves us. Although I am not grateful that I had cancer, I am grateful that God allowed me to travel that road and have true faith in Him that all would be good.

"And I want you to know dear brothers and sisters , that everything that has happened to me here has helped to spread the Good News."

—Philippians 1:12 (NLT)

Day Seven

Hello, Monday! I was truly grateful for the weekend! Although we just stayed in and rested, it felt nice just being together as we were trying to figure out my food situation. I was still having a hard time with nausea and smells, and most of my food intake consisted of saltines, turkey, and applesauce.

Mondays were not my favorite day, but I was still learning to take it one day at a time without thinking about tomorrow or next week. My radiation treatments were a little earlier that week. As I entered through the doors toward the treatment area, I placed all my clothes in a locker. Then I proceeded to put on my cute gown, all the while praying for peace. My team then brought me into the radiation room where I removed my boots and hopped onto the table. One of them gently handed me the dilator to insert into my vagina as I was trying to get comfortable. It felt a little more difficult to insert and somewhat uncomfortable, but thankfully it went in. After setting me up, the same routine happened— lots of radiation and so much time to think alone. Trying not to let my thoughts go to a negative place, I continually said that prayer, which always brought me some peace. I knew God was always there with me. Otherwise I would have jumped off the table and said, "I am done!"

Have you ever felt that way? Quietly saying to yourself, "You are done!" Done with feeling sad, done with feeling alone, done with feeling hurt, done with feeling not appreciated, and done with cancer! I have felt that way, but I knew I wasn't done. I had to face it daily. As King David said, "The troubles of my heart enlarged; bring me out of my distresses" (Psalms 25:17).

So, how do you endure it all?

Jesus promised that His people will experience pain and turmoil on earth, but He makes clear that whatever pain and suffering we endure, the prize in the end is God allowing us to have a relationship with Him through Jesus Christ, we will benefit and God will receive all the glory.

The true reality is, we may never heal. Sometimes sickness is just the reality of a broken world. I don't have to be healed to put my trust in Him. My hope is in who God is—- His character. He has proven it over and over again.

The doors slowly opened—always a beautiful sight! I loved watching them come to my rescue! They always said, "Okay, we're done!" After each session, I used the bathroom, slowly got dressed, and thanked God for getting me through another day.

As I entered the waiting room and noticed William sitting in the chair, reading, as always, I was grateful that he was with me and helped me get through the day-to-day treatments. I could always share my thoughts and feelings with him while I was going through each one. In those moments, strong faith got us through the difficult times when our minds wandered off into fear.

I couldn't spend much time in God's word because it was hard to focus when my mind and body was not feeling well. I was too busy trying to stay alive. But every moment I read some Scriptures, I knew He had led me into His presence to receive a love letter filled with His promises. Something wonderful happens whenever I read God's word: my faith grows stronger and I can endure any circumstance.

The Bible is full of promises for healing. David said, "Bless the Lord, O my soul, and forget not all his benefits, who forgives all your iniquity, who heals all your diseases"(Psalm 103:2-3).Thank you, God!

"You shall love the Lord your God with all your heart and with all your soul and with all your strength and with all your mind, and your neighbor as yourself."

—Luke 10:27 (ESV)

Day Eight

Good morning, Tuesday! I was a bit restless through the night, but eating a few crackers and ginger ale helped me sleep. Even still, I was often lying awake with my mind on overdrive.

I believed this was all happening for a reason. This unexpected diagnosis of cancer reminded me that every day is a blessing. I felt a deep desire to worship God more—*truly worship Him*—and honor Him more. With each moment, I tried the best I could, but I still had a hard time focusing...and it was getting even harder. Thankfully I prayed often and felt His comfort. It's amazing that once I hit a *crisis* I really started to listen to God. He gave me the grace to handle all of it.

As I looked over to the writing desk in our hotel room, I noticed William writing a beautiful letter to God in his journal, which he had been doing for so many years. What a precious gift to Him. I appreciate William so much every day. How special it was to share every moment with my spouse. This may not have been my most favorite time or experience, but I appreciate sharing it all with him. I knew he was worried about me and needed to ask God to heal me. With both of us praying, I knew God was helping me even more. I felt His love and I felt William's love. I am so grateful!

By this point in my treatments, my body was feeling tired most of the time and my energy a bit depleted. I tried to save all my energy for walking to and from the treatments. I found it quite amazing that my body could handle all it was being put through. The Bible tells us to pray for everything, which includes healing. It does not promise our present bodies will stay healthy and last forever.

My radiation oncologist was wonderful and so was his nurse! She lightened the mood and I was always happy to see her! They always did a quick rectal check to see how my skin was doing and offered some help. My skin was changing and my bowels were changing too. I was trying to give my skin the best care with lotions and trying to eat whatever the nutritionist suggested to help my bowels, as I was beginning to have a lot of diarrhea. My nutritionist suggested I begin the BRAT diet: bananas, rice, applesauce, and toast. So I began supplementing that with crackers because I still couldn't eat toast.

I was always feeling a bit nauseous, but I was able to deal with it. Before I headed off to bed that night, William and I said a special prayer for the day. We both have a beautiful feeling of love for God and want to continue to praise and honor Him always. We continue to worship Him. We feel the presence of true joy, *despite my circumstances.*

How is it possible to have joy *now?* Maybe not in the same way as Paul writes in Philippians 4:4 "rejoice always." He is writing these words while in prison. We are not talking about circumstantial joy, but spiritual joy, which has nothing to do with our circumstances. It is a joy based on the Lord. It's a constant peace that remains in our hearts. "Keep your eyes on Jesus, who both began and finished the race we're in. Study how he did it. Because He never lost sight of where He was headed- that exhilarating finish in and with God. And, now he's there, in the place of honor, right alongside God" (Hebrews 12:2).

God gave us all a new life when we accepted Jesus Christ as our Savior. Paul wants believers to be filled with a Christ-filled life. "Be filled with the fruit of righteousness that comes through Jesus Christ, to the glory and praise of God." (Philippians 1:11).

*"And we know that God causes
everything to work together
for the good of those who love
God and are called according
to His purpose for them."*

—Romans 8:28 (NLT)

Day Nine

It was Wednesday! Another great day! I woke up a little later because my stomach was feeling quite nauseous and I had been restless all night. I spent a lot of time on the toilet that morning, so you know what that means—my diarrhea was getting much worse. I was having bowel movements at least five times a day.

My parents stayed with me while William went home to Florida to spend time with our son, Michael. We had made reservations early for Michael to come home for Thanksgiving break from college. Who would have thought I would have been at Sloan Kettering in New York receiving treatment for cancer? This certainly was not *my* plan. Sometimes we feel our plans are better than what God has planned for our life. God's plans are bigger than our plan. God is our Father and He knows our thoughts and needs. He always gives us a choice, including if we will trust in Him. Through His Word, God speaks to us and reminds us that He is faithful.

Michael wanted to come to New York to see me, but I thought it would be better for him to see his friends and enjoy his time rather than being in a small hotel where his mom spends most of her time in the bathroom and just lying around. Selfishly, I didn't want him seeing me like that. No one is ever prepared to see how their parent is dealing with all the symptoms that come with treatment. Looking back, I should have switched his flight to be with me, but I wanted what I thought was best for him. I knew he would be home in a few weeks for winter break anyway, and I was definitely going to be home for that!

My parents were so wonderful to walk with me to and from my treatments in the cold weather! I knew it wasn't easy for them, but they never complained. They continuously are by my side and always offer their love and support. They just showed up. Sometimes when you go through a critical time in your life, you need people around you to help. How do you help someone in need? The Bible commands us to" love your neighbor as yourself" (Mark 12:31). You just show up and spend time with them. I needed their love and support and they never gave up. My parents are committed to stand strong and fight for me.

God is the one who *actually* fights the battle. I am in good hands with the love and support of God. We need to believe John15:5 which says that we cannot do anything apart from God. We have a choice. We can continue to do it our way or we can recognize that the battle is the Lord's (2 Chronicles 20:15). The battle is God's, but the victory is ours.

William called to inform me that our daughter, Courtney, and Michael helped him decorate our house for Christmas! I was so happy that I cried! I know how much time and effort it takes to put up Christmas trees, garland, and all the other *stuff* we have to decorate our home. Maybe I cried because I wasn't there for the entire process of planning out our Christmas home decorations. Either way, I knew I would be home for Christmas!

My parents and I watched some Hallmark Christmas movie that night and went to bed around 10:45.

Thank you God...for another day!

"And let the peace of Christ rule in your hearts, to which indeed you were called on one body. And be thankful."

—*Colossians 3:15 (ESV)*

Day Off

Happy Thanksgiving! I am so thankful for God and all His blessings, namely William; the rest of my family, and friends! I am also grateful to my doctors, nurses, and all the people who have been involved in my journey! Today, I have peace. Whenever I feel some sort of despair, I cling onto the verse John 16:33, where Jesus spoke to his followers, "I have said these things to you, that in me you may have peace. In the world you will have tribulation. But take heart; I have overcome the world." When I continue to let God into my heart, I hold on to that peace.

I have always loved Joni Eareckson Tada and have been encouraged by her faith. She is a beautiful Christian woman who became a quadriplegic after diving into the Chesapeake Bay when she was 17 years old. She sank into deep depression after her accident, but she began to trust God more every day. She loves Jeremiah 29:11, "For I know the plans I have for you, declares the Lord, plans to give you hope and a future." As a quadriplegic she didn't receive the healing of walking, using her body, or her hands, but instead she received a deeper healing of the soul. As she was pushed into the arms of God every day, she cried out to Jesus, "I can't do this thing called life. I need your strength. I can't make it through the day." She has experienced the sweetest, most precious union with Christ. "Finding Jesus in our hell on earth makes life worth it."

The nights were always tough because I was always twisting and turning. My mind was always racing with *thoughts;* I was always trying to keep them positive, but some of those negative ones crept in. So I continued to pray to make me feel better. God always tells us not to be anxious for anything, but pray in everything. Every time I started worrying or becoming anxious, I knew that's when I needed to read God's words, to fill my mind with God's truths and scripture.

Even on my day off I spent a lot of time in the bathroom, and it was getting a bit painful. By this time, I was unable to wipe anymore because my skin had become so sensitive in my buttocks area. So after my bowel movements, I had to use warm water to soothe my skin and dab with a towel instead of using toilet paper.

We decided to stay in that day because it was only 20 degrees outside. I was thrilled that we had bought extra food the day before to have a small turkey dinner... well, more like deli turkey with my crackers, while my parents ate a hot open-faced turkey sandwich with mashed potatoes and corn. At that point, we didn't care what kind of food we were consuming on Thanksgiving. We were just happy to be together.

I spoke with all our children that day as well. We usually spoke most days, but for obvious reasons talking to them was even more special on Thanksgiving. William and I are grateful to God for these most precious gifts.

William called me from Florida to inform me he had gone food shopping with Michael the day before to buy a turkey and all the sides. He said Michael wanted to try to make Thanksgiving dinner for them since I wasn't there to cook. That touched my heart. I thought they were going out to a restaurant to eat dinner, but I knew Michael is a good cook, especially when he cooks steaks!

So Michael attempted to cook the turkey, but he said it didn't turn out so well. So they ate mashed potatoes, stuffing, and vegetables and had deli turkey just like my parents and I did. I was so proud of him because he tried!

All in all, my day off was a great day and I am so thankful that my family was able to spend this wonderful day with us, both in New York and in Florida!

"*I will praise the name of God with a song; I will magnify Him with Thanksgiving.*"

—Psalm 69:30 (ESV)

Day Ten

It was finally Friday! I was feeling a little *down* that day, but my parents spent time with me in the city. Maybe I was down because William wasn't there with me and I was so used to being with him all the time. I knew he would be back Sunday, though, so I was looking forward to that!

Since it was Friday, I had the weekend off from chemo and radiation. Maybe I was just tired of feeling sick and having bowel movements all day, every day, and not being able to eat anything I enjoy. But I was trying to stay positive and not think about it. I never discussed anything negative with anyone, not even with William. We never discussed *cancer* or my treatments. "One day at a time" was my motto to get through this.

But this day was different. My mother woke up feeling energized and wanted to clean our hotel room, or at least make up the pull-out bed into a couch once again. She then proceeded to say, "Let's all get dressed early and we'll go to Pottery Barn or some store nearby just to browse."

Sounds good to me, I thought. *Maybe after I get some fresh air, I'll get back to myself.* So I got dressed and once again just brushed the ends of my hair like I'd been doing, put on some makeup, went to the bathroom about six times, and then I was ready to go. The funny part was my mother said to me, "Do you want to curl your hair a little?"

I almost laughed because that's usually not my mom. She normally doesn't care how I look, and I am the one who always likes to *dress up.* But while I was in treatment, that didn't mean much to me. I wanted to keep as much hair as possible on my head, so to apply some hot curling iron to it was definitely not happening. I politely said, "No, I'm fine."

Sometimes grief, loss, or a *diagnosis of cancer* removes the desire to take care of yourself. You try to function as *normal* as possible, but it doesn't feel the same. The only thing that matters at the time is how you are feeling and trying to *survive.* You pick yourself up each day, take a shower, put on a little makeup and continue to walk out the door *almost motionless.*

I look to the Scriptures for encouragement and hope. "That through endurance and through encouragement of the Scriptures we might have hope (Romans 15:4). God's word teaches us the principles for the path to peace. Worshipping God and trusting in Him for whatever happens in my life, good or bad, will bring me peace.

All of a sudden, our doorbell rang. I opened the door and it was our daughter, Courtney. I was so happy to see her! Courtney lives in Miami and chose to fly out that day because the flights were less expensive the day after Thanksgiving and spend the entire day with us!

We all went to my treatment together and had an early dinner. Unfortunately, I could only order a baked potato because of my limited BRAT diet, but I would add eggs and turkey for protein.

We all enjoyed having Courtney around. She brought some games like Yahtzee and Clue for us to play. We had the best night, just laughing!

God brings people into our lives when we *really* need them. That day, God knew I needed to see Courtney to cheer me up. I know God has His perfect timing for us and He delivers. That day, He delivered my daughter. Who knows what He will deliver another day? Thank you, God, for this wonderful gift!

"Yet God had made everything beautiful for its own time. He has planted eternity in the human heart, but even so, people cannot see the whole scope of God's work from beginning to end."

—Ecclesiastes 3:1 (NLT)

Day Eleven

Monday again! What a wonderful weekend we all had together with Courtney! We went to Madame Tussauds wax museum and had so much fun taking pictures with the famous wax people. This was the first time in a couple of weeks I actually felt *normal*. I just wanted to feel like myself and do some regular activities. Staying home, especially in a hotel for so long, gets lonely and I was beginning to feel isolated since I didn't feel well enough to go out and enjoy Manhattan.

We had to limit our time while we were out because my body was getting more tired more easily. My parents and Courtney ordered dinner in from a local restaurant. The meal looked absolutely delicious! It sure would have been nice to eat that instead of my usual turkey with crackers and some cranberry juice with water.

I didn't want to start having a *pity party* about my food intake. Quickly, I snapped out of it and maintained a positive attitude during treatment. It is important to emphasize that you can have moments of sadness and frustration, and *fear*. I have felt all of those emotions. I just felt better when I kept a positive outlook on everything. I want to continue to be full of joy and peace while I am seeking treatment.

William arrived on Sunday, so we all decided to see a Broadway show. Florida offered some shows, but nothing like Broadway.

Since Courtney was still in town, she came to my treatment, along with William, and it went so much better, especially considering it was a Monday. My parents had left the day before, after William arrived home. I'm sure they were thrilled to sleep in their own bed instead of the pull-out couch at the hotel.

When Courtney left to return to Miami, we were so sad to see her go, but so happy she came. It truly made my weekend.

Treatments were getting increasingly harder to deal with. As wonderful as it was to spend time with William and my family, I still needed God's help to get through this. I still had hope. I still understood that my road would be difficult but that one day I would receive the Kingdom of God. I know that all these struggles in this human life will never compare to that glory of heaven. No matter how bleak it felt sometimes, I knew God would get us through it. Thank you, God!

"The Lord gives strength to his people; the Lord blesses his people with peace."

—Psalm 29:11 (NIV)

Day Twelve

Hello, Tuesday! I woke up early and off I went to the bathroom. I had been spending a lot of time there.

Walking through the cancer treatment taught me many lessons, *which I always needed.* I know that God is more interested in my character than my comfort, so I will deal with the discomfort in order to learn about my character. James 1:3 says, "For when your faith is tested your endurance has a chance to grow." God has already recorded every test in the Bible. We just have to read His word to discover how people got through each test. Focusing on God's greatness and all of His promises, thanking Him for those promises, and asking Him to take care of me and heal me got me through each day. When we take the focus off ourselves and put it on God, we can relax.

We were not placed on earth to have an *easy* life, and it's not about us. We are here on earth to strengthen our character for heaven, which the Holy Spirit has the power to do. I worship God not for my benefit, but to bring glory to Him.

From a human perspective, being comfortable and living without difficult times makes sense. But from a Christian standpoint, we know that we will experience trouble in this life. Jesus says, "I have said these things to you, that you may have peace. In the world you will have tribulation. But take heart; I have overcome the world" John 16:33. Jesus experienced intense suffering, but it was for God's purpose. He was providing a way to salvation for all of us and He would be glorified.

Our heavenly Father is orchestrating everything together for our good. The word *everything* means even the difficult things that happens to us. When the Apostle Paul was in prison for two years, he wrote the letter to the Philippians proclaiming the kingdom of God and sharing about Jesus Christ. Despite his circumstances, Paul found ways to share the good news. These are all good lessons for me to learn. Whatever our situation is, we should learn to be joyful and give God all the glory.

My life here on earth looks different and *feels* different. And, so does my eternal life in heaven. Jesus said, "I am going to prepare a place for you" (John 14:2). How grateful I am for Jesus. And, how much I have come to know and love him more every day.

All of our sufferings and hurts will disappear once we enter heavens gates. When I think of earth and all of its beauty whether it is the natural landscape, to spectacular views, my thoughts are fixed on human beings. We are individually born perfect and beautiful in the eyes of God.

And, when I think about heaven, it is reality. I want you to have hope and know that "Jesus is the way, the truth and the life" (John 14:6). Heaven is a matter of faith. According to Philippians 3:20, "our citizenship is in heaven." Having true faith is believing something you hope for and trusting in God what he has to say about heaven from his Word.

So, now I will humbly thank God, *in advance*, for whenever my time is ready to "go home."

"Not only that, but we rejoice in our sufferings, knowing that suffering produces endurance, and endurance produces character, and character produces hope, and hope does not put us to shame, because God's love has been poured into our hearts through the Holy Spirit who has been given to us."

—Romans 5:3–5 (ESV)

Day Thirteen

Wednesday! As I walked through this difficult season, I faced many different situations, each with a specific lesson. I learned to *be still* and reflect on who God is: our refuge, strong and helpful when we are weak. So I will continue to be quiet and praise Him in my weakest moments. Although there have been times in my life when I felt that God didn't hear my prayers and He felt so far away, God didn't leave me during those times. He did not promise we will *feel* His presence; instead He promised in Hebrews 13:5, "I will never leave you nor forsake you." I have now learned to *trust* God instead of *feeling* Him near.

One of the side effects of chemotherapy is a loss of appetite. It was easier for me to eat little and often instead of large main meals. Everything tasted a bit different, but I was getting used to my *new* normal. I found that pretzels settled my stomach even more than crackers. A bit of ginger ale was good, as well.

Most of my mornings were still spent in the bathroom, followed by afternoons of treatment, taking showers, applying creams, eating, and taking chemo pills. Although it sounds daunting, I *felt* encouraged that all would be good.

After my showers, I slipped into anything that kept me warm. William and I cuddled mostly in bed because I could stretch out on it, and on the couch. I tried to read, but my mind didn't allow me to focus, so I just sat with the television on and watched shows that were positive and happy. I was sure William was getting bored with my choices of programs, but he didn't complain.

I am grateful for my relationship with William. It's reassuring to know that he has my best interest at heart. And, I am there for him. While in treatment, I was unable to be myself, but he understood completely. William was looking beyond his own happiness and instead looking to find ways to comfort me when I *really* needed him. During my difficult moments, his love was one of the greatest gifts of all.

"I will never fail you. I will never abandon you."

—Hebrews 13:5 (NLT)

Day Fourteen

Hello, Thursday! While trying to relax in bed, I learned that God has the power to offer us incredible peace despite our circumstances. In the New Testament, Paul said, "Now may the Lord of peace himself give you peace at all times in every way. The Lord be with you all" (2 Thessalonians 3:16). We get to know who God is during the desperate moments. We learn to hold on to God when we really need Him.

While I was receiving treatment, my mind drifted off and caused me to worry, but when I asked God for peace, I *felt* His presence. Those were the days that increased my faith in God. Whatever you're dealing with, you are not alone, and God can help you. As Romans 8:28 tells us, "All things work together for good." When something happens to us that makes us feel uncomfortable or doesn't happen the way we want it to happen, we can have faith that God will work that situation out for good.

Our youngest daughter, Ashley, called that morning, and I told her I was doing well and staying strong. It was a good opportunity to let her know how much I needed God's strength to get me through my treatments. I wanted her to know that whenever she is having a difficult time that she will always seek God for His strength. Wouldn't it be wonderful if our children never experienced pain or difficult times? Yes, but that's life.

William and I met with my nutritionist once again. She felt I was eating well and staying on track. She also didn't seem too concerned about my daily episodes of diarrhea, as it was normal for the kind of treatment I was enduring, and it could have been due to the chemo pills or the radiation.

I'd lost a few pounds, but that was to be expected. I tried to eat as often as possible, but *every time something went in...then it went out.*

The dilator used for my radiation treatment was becoming increasingly difficult to enter and it hurt! Thankfully, everyone in the radiation department was extremely helpful.

On our walk home, William usually stopped at the deli next to the hospital to buy a fresh salad for himself. Oh, how I would have loved to have eaten a salad! I was craving lettuce, tomatoes, cucumbers, and avocado! But since I couldn't eat it, I just tried not to think about it too much. I found sticking to my prescribed diet difficult at times because I had to keep eating the same meals. My nutritionist said I could have some yogurt, so that's what I would eat for a snack. I was also still trying to drink as much water as possible, but it still made me pretty nauseous, so I added a little cranberry juice to make it more *tasteful.*

"For God so loved the
world, that He gave his only
Son, that whoever believes
in him should not perish,
but have eternal life."

—John 3:16 (ESV)

Day Fifteen

Friday was a special day because the doorman knocked on our front door and handed me the most beautiful bouquet of yellow roses from a dear friend who knew that yellow roses signified friendship, joy, and well wishes. I absolutely loved the flowers, but more than that, I loved the kindness and thoughtfulness behind those flowers.

Relationships are the key to happiness. In order to be happy, we need special bonds with people. When we are facing difficult moments, we need support from people who care and love us. *Those little sweet notes I have received from family members and friends make my day.*

Life is so much more precious to me than it has ever been. When I look back on my life, it's easy to see I didn't always do the right thing. I made up excuses not to act quickly on things that could have helped someone. One of my favorite verses is Proverbs 3:27, which says, "Do not withhold good from those to whom it is due, when it is in your power to do it." Every day God gives us small tests to practice kindness. When we have the opportunity to help someone, we should do it.

Life can be difficult and wonderful at the same time. William and I have been blessed with four children, who mean the world to us and who we would do anything for. They truly have our hearts and we are always thinking about them even though they are all adults ranging in age from 21-27. We cherish our time with them even more now because they all live away from home. I tried not to *worry* about them when they were growing up, but William and I always wanted to keep them safe and healthy.

Now that they are adults we pray they have true joy in their lives and that they make good decisions daily, ones that honor God. We pray they can love others and share their lives with wonderful friends and spouses who love God and respect them.

Once again, I saw my colorectal oncologist to check my bloodwork and vitals. The bloodwork came back fairly normal. Some areas were a little low, but nothing of real concern. My heart rate was still fast, but the doctor was fine with all of my stats. He did suggest Imodium, however, to stop the diarrhea.

Later that afternoon, I spoke with a few friends on the phone. Anytime one of my friends asked how I was doing, my usual answer was "good" because it was difficult for me to discuss my day-to-day routine. Discussing the *actual* treatment I was receiving somehow made me feel more nervous and anxious, but I found writing about my feelings much better than discussing them with others.

Some family members and friends were probably wondering, *Is she really good?* and *I guess treatment is not so bad?* For the record, my treatments were emotionally, physically, and mentally draining, but our God walked beside me every day...every hour...every minute.

*"This is my commandment,
that you love one another
as I have loved you."*

—John 15:12 (ESV)

Day Sixteen

Monday! William and I spent the weekend relaxing... well, at least I did. William always went for his daily walks through New York City and did all the grocery shopping. He also bought some panties for me, which I desperately needed. Instead of thongs, which were my norm, thanks to William, I was now wearing cute bikini panties with *normal* coverage. I had forgotten what it was like to wear a whole panty.

My sweet William also did all our laundry. Thankfully, the hotel had a washer and dryer on our floor. I was usually the laundry queen at home, but I truly appreciated his help during a time when I had no strength to do the *normal* things in life.

Took my chemo pills in the morning and then William and I walked to and from treatment in the beautiful, but chilly weather. We still missed our home and the wonderful weather in Florida. We always tried to remain positive, but there were many days I *wanted* to have more space and walk around the comfort of my home. I loved the smell of my house. I missed watching television in my living room. I missed my own pots and pans. I missed my comfortable robe that I wore in the mornings, which I had forgotten to pack.

Having faith through those difficult times was the only way I got through each day. I quieted my heart during the painful moments when I felt abandoned by God. In Psalm 13, David was on the verge of despair.

"How long, O Lord? Will you forget me forever?" He cannot feel the presence of God and feels like God has ignored his pain and sorrow.

I have felt this way. Many days I have cried out to God asking Him to draw near to me. Let us put our hope in Him even when the darkness will not lift and even when we feel "abandoned" by God. Sing song of praises and worship Him always. He has the power to work some beautiful miracles in our lives. Jesus promises in Matthew 7:7, "Ask, and it will be given to you; seek, and you will find; knock and it will be opened to you." God always wants to bless us.

"For I consider that the sufferings of this present time are not worth comparing with the glory that is to be revealed to us."

—Romans 8:18 (ESV)

Day Seventeen

Tuesday I woke up to my usual bathroom regimen. I was feeling much more sore because the radiation was targeting both my front and rectal areas.

Although I was still feeling quite weak and nauseous, I was trying to eat as often as possible. By this point, pretzels soothed my stomach more than the crackers I had been eating. Ginger ale still helped, but I was able to sip only a teaspoon or two. Drinking water was essential, and although it was difficult when my stomach was queasy, I still somehow managed to swallow it.

Instead of *thinking too much,* I tried to watch television to keep myself busy. William sat near me to watch a few of my feel-good shows, but when TV became too much for him, he would read the Bible or the newspaper. Some days when I needed some extra care, he gave me a massage. Somehow that eased my body and made me feel a little better. When I was pregnant with our children, he gave me a 30-minute massage every day. Maybe that's why I had four children—just kidding! He said he felt lucky that I was carrying our children and a massage was the least he could do.

I asked William if we could take a taxi to the hospital because it was getting harder for me to walk there and the weather was bitterly cold. He looked at me and I could see on his face, *Oh boy, it's really hitting her.* But he said, "Of course, let's get a taxi!" I was thrilled to be able to sit down and be driven to the hospital.

When we arrived at the hospital, it was wonderful to see all my "friends" there. Although those of us in the waiting room did not speak to one another, we sent warm smiles to each other knowing what we were going through together. Some people came and went, but I found it comforting to see many of the same people there every time I went in.

I also heard the comforting sound of patients ringing the bell. The tradition of ringing this bell at the end of a patient's cancer treatment has been in effect since 1996. Every time we heard the ringing of the bell, everyone clapped at the joy of this special moment. Many people were joined by family and friends in celebration. There is even a poem about this special event:

> *Ring this bell*
> *three times well*
> *Its toll to clearly say*
> *My treatment's done*
> *This course is run*
> *And I am on my way!*
>
> —*Irve Le Moyne*

It always made me cry whenever I heard the bell because I could see how happy other patients were that their treatments and their pain were behind them. But I often thought, *Yeah, that will be me one day.*

God says in Jeremiah 29:11, "'For I know the plans I have for you,' declares the LORD, 'plans to prosper you and not to harm you, plans to give you hope and a future.'"

"For God alone my soul waits in silence; from Him comes my salvation."

—Psalms 62:1 (ESV)

Day Eighteen

William and I were awake early on Wednesday and, as usual, I was immediately off to the bathroom. The skin in my lower region continued to become highly sensitive and painful. Plus, my extremely sore hemorrhoids were screaming.

At this point, it didn't matter what I ate because everything affected my bowels. So I prayed for relief and stuck to my BRAT diet.

William and I walked to Sloan even though it was 32 degrees outside. I wanted to get some exercise to rejuvenate my body.

As I walked into the dressing room to put on my gown and get ready for the treatment, I said many more prayers. I was feeling a bit anxious and I needed God's help. I tried to stay calm and ask God for His peace.

Then, as the hospital staff opened the doors to let me in, I suddenly felt a little better. I was greeted by one of the radiation therapists. I hopped onto the table and squirmed to fit inside my mold. I lay down and they moved me around as usual until they found the perfect spot for my radiation. Then they suddenly left and those enormous doors closed behind them. There I was once again, alone in the room, with those huge machines all around me. As I felt that familiar buzzing and zapping sound while the radiation went into my body, I just asked God to help me through it. Every minute seemed so long.

Finally after 30 minutes those doors slowly opened, and I was free. I wanted to jump off the table, but by this point I just tried as best I could to get off the table slowly and thanked them for another day.

While I was thinking about trying to leave, I began to feel so grateful for the entire staff at Sloan Kettering. As God impressed on my heart the role of service to others, I became more thankful for the radiation therapists, doctors, nurses, technicians, nutritionist, and personnel. How can I show my gratefulness for them? How can I maintain true joy in my life? Practicing gratitude gives people the ability to face the challenges while finding joy throughout their struggle. You may send a gratitude letter to the nurses or oncologist. Start a journal and make a list writing down everything you are grateful for. Whatever you choose to be grateful for, there is much love and joy that surrounds you.

As I walked back to the dressing room, there were more patients waiting to be treated, and I'm sure they were all thinking the same thing I was: "I can't wait until this is done!" As usual, I thanked God for getting me through another day. I will always be grateful to God because all the glory, praise, and honor belong to Him.

"*God is our refuge and strength, always ready to help in times of trouble.*"

—*Psalm 46:1 (NLT)*

Day Nineteen

Thursday was quite welcome as I had been feeling anxious and restless all night, which caused lots of tossing and turning. I felt so bad for William because he probably heard me moving around all night and using the bathroom.

We both woke up early to the sound of my alarm. As I mentioned, I like to stay on a schedule. If my doctor said I had to take my chemo pills 12 hours apart, then that's what I was going to do. It seemed a bit too much, but if it made me feel safer to spread them out, then I was going to listen to my doctor.

When William and I were getting dressed for my treatment, I looked in the mirror and tried to brush my hair slightly. It seemed thinner but I was grateful to have any at all. Somehow long, beautiful hair didn't matter. I was just grateful to be healthy. Cancer and the thought of death go hand in hand and every day became more special and more precious.

I knew I needed my Savior, Jesus, to heal me. William and I knew we needed to pray more, so we cried out to Him to help me get through this challenging time. I didn't think I could get through this pain, but I did because of Him.

I am grateful for our pastor, church, and all of the members of the congregation. We are members of a small church and I am grateful for our church friends. Greeting people and friends every week and exchanging hugs warms my heart. I enjoy singing songs about Jesus and reading verses that lifts my spirit. While I missed attending church in treatment, I clung on to the memories of the songs, prayers, and messages. God was with me in the everyday details of my life *right now.*

Thank you, God, for being there with us through that interesting season of life. We appreciate you drawing us closer to you. We love you!

"Jesus told him, 'I am the way, the truth, and the life. No one can come to the Father except through me.'"

—John 14:6 (NLT)

Day Twenty

I had always loved Fridays, but this particular Friday, I was scheduled to have another infusion of chemo. Our daughter, Taylor, and my parents came in to support me. William and I woke up at around 6 a.m. because I had to eat breakfast and pack some food before we left for the hospital. The infusion was at another location on 53rd Street.

I had an inordinately difficult time sleeping through the night since I knew what to expect when I got up that morning. So many scenarios were running through my mind and caused me to become even more anxious than I already was. *Will my body be able to handle even more chemo? How is my heart doing?* After all, I was already taking chemo pills daily and my body felt so weak from all the radiation.

William and I arrived at the hospital at 8:00 a.m. and my parents were already in the waiting room. They were smiling and truly happy to see me, but I knew they were putting on their brave face just like I was. It must have been difficult to watch their daughter receive chemo. My dad was always asking me, "How did you get cancer?"

I wish I'd had an answer for him, but I just said, "I don't know, but with God's help I'm going to beat this."

A few minutes later, a nurse called me in to take my vitals and draw some blood to find out if my levels were normal so I could have an infusion. The nurse noticed my heart rate was rather fast and informed my oncologist, who then suggested an electrocardiogram (EKG). It came back normal.

William and I met with my colorectal oncologist before my infusion to discuss my bloodwork. Everything seemed fine, a little low like before, but good. While I was waiting for my doctor, I had another episode of diarrhea, which continued the entire time I was waiting. So many thoughts were racing through my mind. *How can my body handle any more chemo? Will my heart be able to handle more chemo? Will I have diarrhea while I'm receiving chemo?*

I was probably more anxious that day than I had been because I *really* didn't want any more chemo. This seemed way too much for my body to handle. I remember asking my doctor if I *really* needed to get this infusion and he said, "Yes." So I picked myself up and we all walked together ready to get this thing done.

Prior to this appointment, I had asked for the same nurse that administered the chemo IV the first time. I trusted her and everything turned out well, so thankfully, she was there waiting for me.

As I sat in my reclining chair being hooked up to the IV, I was praying, "Please help me, Lord!" I had an overwhelming need to rely on God's power, strength, and comfort. I clung to God's promises. He is the Great Physician and I needed His comfort right then.

Meanwhile, William and my parents were trying to get my mind off this whole process. They must have sensed I was nervous. It made the day just a little bit *easier.*

When the treatment was over, I was so elated I hugged everyone. Those were the moments I will always remember. As positive and as strong minded as I try to be, I am still weak. That's why I always *need* God. Remember what Paul said in 2 Timothy 2:3, "Endure suffering along with me, as a good soldier of Christ Jesus."

The Good News is the Lord won't leave us there. The *only* thing I could do was pray. I was powerless and I needed God to get me through it. And the support from my family was priceless. How grateful I am!

*"So be strong and courageous!
Do not be afraid and do not
panic before them. For the Lord
your God will personally go
ahead of you. He will neither
fail you nor abandon you."*

—Deuteronomy 31:6 (NLT)

Day Twenty-One

Monday again! The weekend was tough, so I just laid in bed. If I wasn't in the bathroom, I was in bed watching television or trying to rest.

Since I had many episodes of diarrhea, I decided to take an Imodium at my doctor's request. Suddenly, I had a headache, and then I saw these weird prisms. I had never experienced anything like that, so I was thinking, *Oh no, is this it.*

William was out for his walk, so I decided to call my mom because she had experienced some *unusual* occurrences in the past, so I thought she might have an idea of what was happening to me. After I explained the symptoms, she told me I had an ocular migraine, caused by reduced blood flow or spasms of blood vessels in the retina or behind the eye. She told me to close my eyes, go into the bedroom, and lie still. So, quickly I lied on the bed, shut off the lights, and closed my eyes. After a few minutes, I tried to open them and saw no more prisms. My headache was gone and all was good.

Since I had felt extremely ill all weekend, I called my oncologist's nurse because I thought even if I had been able to swallow 5 chemo pills that morning, they would just come up anyway. Thankfully, she told me not to take them but to still go in for radiation. I was grateful, but I was hoping she would also tell me to skip the radiation too. I took an anti-nausea pill, hoping it would help, but I wasn't too sure it did.

I felt so sick that I brought ginger ale and pretzels to my treatment. We took a taxi to and from treatment because it had been a rough couple of days, but I continued to pray even more.

William and I prayed a lot together. We often did, even before my diagnosis, but by this point we were having more "serious" prayers. I know through our most difficult moments that God was always there with us. He didn't take away the pain, but He was *changing* me!

I am grateful for God and I know that was His plan for me. He promised He would never leave me and He would be there through every trial. I love God, truly love God. As Mark 12:30 tells us to do, "Love the Lord your God with all your heart and with all your soul and with all your mind and with all your strength."

"Don't worry about anything;
instead pray about everything.
Tell God what you need, and
thank Him for all He has done."

—Philippians 4:6 (NLT)

Day Twenty-Two

It was Tuesday, the day of my weekly appointment with my radiation oncologist. I started off the morning still feeling nauseous, but a little better. I was back to my usual chemo pills. I was hoping my doctor would say, "Oh, you've taken enough," but I was determined to finish strong.

The weather looked beautiful with temperatures in the 30s. I knew we needed to take a taxi again because I didn't think I could walk to and from the hospital any longer. I didn't need to exert any more energy.

When I arrived, the staff was on time, so they took me immediately. Since it was Tuesday, they usually did more scans, so I was expecting it. I studied everything while I was in there. I knew if the machines were working properly and I knew what to expect. I still had anxious feelings while I was in the radiation room, but I looked to that paint chip on the wall and repeated "I can do all things through Christ who strengthens me!" I am so grateful for that prayer.

I gave thanks to God because I knew He would give me the strength to overcome my situation. I also believed I would grow through this experience if I allowed God to lead me to grow. When times were tough that's when I needed to be reminded all that God has given me—all the people in my life and the good health I had always experienced.

Most people who have experienced any kind of serious illness need consistent friends and family who show up in their lives and let them know, *I am thinking about you and sending well wishes.* I understand it's hard to know what to say when someone has a serious illness like cancer. *I never knew what to say.* Some people may *pull* away from that person because they don't know what to say. What I learned is to personalize well wishes in a card and be a source of encouragement and support to a friend who is suffering.

When we are suffering we want to hear great stories that bring hope and encouragement. When we are full of fear and feeling sick, we are craving for some Good News. Make a choice to think on things that are true, honest, pure, lovely, and just, and say a prayer for your loved one's family members. Renew their minds and keep them encouraged.

One day we will stand before God and He will ask , "Did you fulfill what I put you on earth to do? Did you read my Word? Did you learn to love other people? Gods commands us to "love Him" and "love others." Love is an action. We show love by spending time with God and with people.

Whenever we have the opportunity to show love we should do good. It is the number one goal in life. Jesus said, "This is my commandment, that you love one another as I have loved you" (John 15:12). He loved us because God is love.

*"You will keep in perfect peace
those whose minds are steadfast,
because they trust in you."*

—Isaiah 26:3 (NIV)

Day Twenty-Three

When I sat back and thought about what usually happens on Wednesdays, it sometimes overwhelmed me. Cancer treatments are difficult, but just because *we* have cancer doesn't mean we can't enjoy life. We can still do the things that make us happy. We went to the movies one day and even though I was feeling ill, somehow it lifted my spirit.

Cancer patients have good and bad days. It is like a rollercoaster of feelings. However that person is feeling, offer support whether in personal visits or just phone calls to say "Hello, how are you doing?" Send a card to let that person know you are thinking about them and praying for them. Also, do not be afraid to have fun with them. Cancer patients need to laugh and enjoy life. However you choose to help, love and support can make a huge difference.

I was still connecting with people on a daily basis, mostly God. My relationship with Him gave me the strength, peace, and love to continue with my daily treatments.

I was grateful for Wednesday...pain and all.

"I pray that God, the source of hope, will fill you completely with joy and peace because you trust in Him. Then you will overflow with confident hope through the power of the Holy Spirit."

—Romans 15:13 (NLT)

Day Twenty-Four

Thursday once again, and by this point, I was depending on the grace of God more than ever before. Sometimes I felt so helpless and weak, but God was always there to pick me up and tell me to keep going. In my daily distress, I was certain God heard me and showed me His great love. I knew this great struggle was meant to shape me and not to harm me. As I stood firm, my faith grew. God controls the storm and knows when to stop it.

Through all this pain, I realized how important life is and how much I need my Savior! Jesus sacrificed Himself on the cross for me, and without his death and resurrection, I would face eternal separation from God. I have God's grace and unconditional love, which remains constant.

My relationships were so important throughout my treatments. I appreciated spending time with William, just sitting on the couch and sharing stories. Relationships can bring us joy or sadness, but God wants us to relate to people His way.

Approximately 50 percent of marriages end in divorce. People feel if it doesn't work out, there's always someone better. Another problem is social media. People spend more time on social media than having strong friendships in real life. What does the Bible tell us about relationships? "'Love the Lord your God with all your heart and with all your soul and with all your strength and with all your mind'; and, 'Love your neighbor as yourself.'" (Luke 10:27) This is the reason God created us.

After radiation, I spoke with a nurse about the constant urination and pain. She took my blood pressure and heart rate, *which was still* 112 beats per minute. *S*he looked concerned, but I told her it was *normal* for me.

The radiation oncologist suggested a cream for my rectal area, which soothed the area where I had lost skin from the radiation. I was surprised after the first week that there was no sign of my pubic hair regrowing. The radiation therapist said, "You are getting laser treatment."

I said, "Yes, I knew there was something good in this."

I continued to take my Imodium pills to stop the diarrhea, but it wasn't working anymore. Although it was painful, I enjoyed that my body was still working sufficiently to get rid of all the *bad* stuff.

My body was getting weaker every day, but *I was fine with that* because I had a deeper sense of peace that surpassed all understanding. Although my body was weak my heart felt strong, and my faith felt even stronger. I was beginning to feel more *courage* and less fear, perhaps because I was trusting God even when I didn't know what was next. I just knew God was always near.

Each time he said, "My grace is all you need. My power works best in weakness." So now I am glad to boast about my weakness, so that the power of Christ can work through me."

—2 Corinthians 12:9 (NLT)

Day Twenty-Five

I was so grateful for Friday, *one day at a time!* I knew I could get through another day—praise God!

What a beautiful blessing every day has been for me! You may be thinking, *What? You were diagnosed with cancer and you had all these treatments and now you are saying it was all a beautiful blessing?* Well, maybe not the treatments, but the people I met: the doctors, the nurses, the nutritionist, and the radiation therapists.

HOPE means Hold On Pain Ends! I used to believe hope was just wishful thinking. *The biblical definition is "confident expectation."* Hope is faith in the future tense: it is a confidence and not just wishful thinking. In Hebrews 11:1, "Now faith is the assurance of things hoped for, the conviction of things not seen." In order for us to have faith, we must be loyal to God. But without hope, life has no meaning. Hope is an enduring virtue of the Christian faith.

Although I continued to have my diarrhea, major hemorrhoids, extreme pain, and nausea, *I was still doing well.*

At this point, I was unable to *sit* properly in the taxi to and from radiation because of the effects of the treatments. Instead I had to lean on my side. I was also spending much more time lying in bed and watching my *happy* shows!

Thank you, God...for another day.

⤳⟋⟍⤲

"They went right into the house
where he was staying, and
Jesus asked them, 'Do you
believe I can make you see?'
'yes, Lord,' they told him,
'we do.' Then he touched their
eyes and said, 'Because of
your faith, it will happen.'"

—Matthew 9:28-29 (NLT)

⤳⟋⟍⤲

Day Twenty-Six

The weekend was extremely difficult. I forgot to mention William recently purchased a Sitz bath for me. This is the *only* comfort someone going through rectal cancer treatments will receive. My hemorrhoids were out of control, and lots of bowel movements.

Before this little Sitz bath I took many showers throughout the day because using the toilet and wiping was much too painful. Everything there was inflamed.

I spent most of my day in bed, other than when I went to the bathroom or ate. William had taken over for me in the kitchen too. Even though he doesn't like to cook, he was extremely helpful in preparing my meals at a time I did not have enough strength or energy to make anything for myself. Believe me, I tried, but it had just become much too difficult.

We definitely took a taxi to the hospital, even though sitting properly was even more difficult because everything hurt. But I appreciated the ride instead of walking.

Before the hospital staff called me in for my radiation treatment, I had another bout of diarrhea and couldn't stop. One of the therapists checked on me and I explained my situation. She called my radiation oncologist and he informed them I needed to continue the treatment. Oh, how I prayed that day. I needed God more than ever. I didn't know how my body would feel anymore.

I walked into the radiation room and one of my usual therapists said to me, "It's amazing you're still smiling and your disposition hasn't changed."

I told him, "Thank you...and that was God." As difficult as it was for me that day, God let people see I was fine.

After my treatment, I spoke to one of the nurses and asked her if I could get a stronger medication cream for my hemorrhoids. A doctor prescribed it for me and I was going to try it when I arrived back at our hotel.

They also prescribed some pain medication for me, but it gave me constipation. I had a tough decision to make. I don't usually like to take medication. *I may just stick to Tylenol,* I thought.

Every day was difficult, both mentally and physically, but I always had HOPE. Hope lies in our souls to turn to God and believe His promises are true.

"Those who hope in the Lord will renew their strength. They will soar on wings like eagles; they will run and not grow weary, they will walk and not be faint."

—Isaiah 40:31 (NIV)

Day Twenty-Seven

This was my last day of treatment...PRAISE GOD!

Thank you, God, for always being there with me *one day at a time*! I know I made it to this day because of you! I will forever be grateful.

How can I express my gratitude toward my loved ones? The words "thank you" don't seem enough, but I am grateful for the love of my family and friends.

Oh my...I had almost no words for the way I was feeling that day. William and I packed up because I made a reservation for us to fly out that evening. I was looking forward to going home and being with my family again.

Our daughter, Taylor, came to our hotel that morning to be with me. She is such a sweet young lady and I love her so much! My parents also met us at the hospital to support me.

Everyone at the hospital, the people who checked me in and my radiation therapists, were wonderful. I walked into the dressing room for the last time and tears just fell down my face—*happy tears!* I thanked God for every moment and asked Him for one more day. I walked into the radiation room and all my radiation therapists were there for me. They prepared me the same way they always had. By this point, it was more painful than ever to get the dilator in, but I did it.

As I lied there on the table, receiving my last treatment, I was thanking God for all of it. I was still saying my prayers and I was still praying I would make it one more day. "I can do all things through Christ who strengthens me." Those 30 minutes were so hard. Every minute I heard the radiation buzzing and entering my body, and it made me shake. As always, I tried not to *think* about it and just kept on praying. I just lied there and took the entire process in. I made it—27 days of radiation!

When those doors opened for the last time...I was overjoyed. I wanted to cry so loudly, but all I could do was smile, and we all just hugged one another. It was such a beautiful moment. I appreciated all of them being there for me.

As I slowly got dressed to walk out of the room for the last time, I just cried. I walked over to my family and we hugged and cried. They all knew how difficult it had been for me because they had been there through it all.

I was about to ring the bell, signifying the end of my treatment. I had been looking forward to ringing this bell since the first day. *I dreamt about it.* I rang it so hard and loud. I just cried and went into the arms of William, Taylor, and my parents.

I met with my radiation oncologist for the last time to discuss my follow-up plan. We said our goodbyes to everyone at Sloan Kettering and left the building. I am truly grateful for all they did for me.

Finally, we took an Uber to the airport. I was going home to see my wonderful family. I have a fear of flying, but at that moment, my fear was gone. I was done with treatment. Thank you, God. We did it.

We arrived at the airport, checked in, and waited to board our flight. We'd had enough time to eat, and although I'd packed a turkey sandwich, it was nowhere to be found. I had put my pocketbook on the conveyer belt and airport security had emptied my bag. I guess they accidentally got rid of my sandwich when they were taking things out. William was concerned because he knew I needed to eat something before we got on the plane. Thankfully, they offered sandwiches at the airport, so we purchased one that was plain with no mayonnaise or mustard on it. I didn't need to upset my stomach even more than it was.

It was a little difficult sitting on the plane with my seatbelt on because I had to sit sideways. No one noticed. William and I looked at one another and just smiled.

When we arrived in Florida, our son, Michael, picked us up. We were all so happy to see him. I'd brought my last chemo pills on the plane and took them.

Finally, we were home, and our two daughters, Ashley and Courtney, had decorated the house with banners, balloons, and streamers. It was so beautiful and I was so happy to be home.

We all hugged one another, and I knew everything was going to be good. I was home with ALL of my family!

Most of all, I would like to thank God! I know this *cancer* has been a blessing to me. For me, I turned to Jesus! Every day, while receiving treatment I clung to the verse, "I can do all things through Jesus Christ who strengthens me." Jesus is the one who was sustaining me. We all need a Savior who saves us from this world and allows us to live with peace and joy with God for *all eternity.* Romans 6:13 says, "Give yourselves completely to God—every part of you…to be tools in the hands of God, to be used for his good purposes." Jesus promised that God would give us all we need if we live for Him and make the Kingdom of God our main purpose.

"For to me, to live is Christ, and to die is gain."

—*Philippians 1:21 (NIV)*

Recovery

I always had hope when I came home...hope that God was always with me. My life has *changed* forever.

The recovery part has been the toughest trial I have ever faced, but I am truly grateful for being able to recover in our home. William and I love sleeping in our bed and waking up to the sounds of our four adult children just talking and laughing all day long.

I am in constant pain *every minute of the day.* My bottom area has no skin left, and going to the bathroom is excruciating. I hold my hands over my eyes and just pray. I don't make any sounds or cry because I don't want to go there. Part of me just wants to cry and the other part wants to scream in pain. But nothing happens because I am always praying, "Please God, don't let it hurt so bad. Help me get through this." I am extremely grateful when it is over, and I thank God *every* time.

I use my Sitz bath seven times a day. I don't know what I would do without it.

My only pain relief is Tylenol. Every third day or so, I take half a dose of pain medicine when I cannot handle the pain anymore. I'm more afraid of the constipation than the pain. So every 6 hours, I take Tylenol and I continue to take it all through the night.

William and I are thrilled to have our children home. I felt sad not being able to do *things* with them. They enjoy sitting on the couch with me and talking or watching a movie. They all love to cook and they take turns preparing a meal. They understand my "diet," so I have my usual. The best moments are spent eating together with me on the couch, sitting side saddled, and them eating around me.

William and I were extremely excited about having Christmas Eve dinner together with everyone. That evening I was feeling pretty bad, but I decided to take a shower and blow dry whatever hair I had left on my head. I applied some makeup, curled my hair a little bit, and put on a red dress. That made me *feel* better.

We all sat around our dining room table and shared such beautiful moments together. Actually I stood the entire meal, but I was able to eat some chicken and mashed potatoes.

Then my entire family went to Christmas Eve service while I stayed home with my parents. I wished they would have gone with everyone, but it was nice to have them home with me.

When everyone arrived home, they told me about the great service and the lighting of the candles while they all sang "Silent Night."

Christmas was wonderful. For the first time *in my* life, presents didn't matter. At that time of the year, I was usually running around trying to find the perfect gifts for everyone because I thought that was what was *important* to me and to my family. But the true meaning of Christmas is celebrating Jesus's birth. The idea of a Christmas gift comes from the Three Wise Men's gifts for Jesus, but that Christmas, I truly enjoyed my family without running around to buy the best presents.

Celebrating Jesus's birth was God's gift to us. We learned that Christmas is about keeping Christ at the center of everything that we do.

After two weeks of constant pain, I had developed some tiny boils on my neck. At first, it started with electrical currents going through the back of my head, like a zapping feeling. I thought it may have been another side effect from the radiation, but I remembered a friend of mine had similar tiny boils on her skin.

I knew it was Shingles because my immune system had been affected and my body was struggling. So my doctor put me on antiviral medication for 10 days.

This was getting even tougher for me, so I cried out to God and asked Him to give me the strength to get through ALL of this! I was not yet healed from my rectal issues and now I had Shingles. I wanted to cry, *and sometimes I did,* but all I could do was pray. Although it was extremely difficult to process, God gave me the strength to endure it all.

From early morning until nighttime, I would read and write on my computer. The Bible was most important because I needed to hear from God and His Word. I would turn on Christian songs and have peaceful moments of worship while praying, reading, and writing.

Finally, after a month of Shingles, I started to feel better. At six weeks, I decided to see my doctor to make sure all was clear. I needed to get my hair done. I wanted *to feel* normal. Can you believe the only time I left the house in 6 weeks was for that one doctor's appointment?

My doctor gave me the best news: I was allowed to get my hair colored. So I called my hairdresser immediately and made an appointment. When I arrived at the salon we all hugged one another. It was so sweet because everyone there told me they had been praying for me. I love them all! My hair stylist is a magician because she gave me the perfect hair color and extensions. My hair loss was fairly significant, so I needed to add more fullness and length.

Recovery has been difficult for me and I'm sure most people who have gone through similar treatments understand. My body still feels weak, but I am able to eat most everything now. I have been craving pizza for 5 months, so William brought home my first pizza pie! He smiled at me as I ate it probably because I made so many weird groaning noises of enjoyment while eating just one slice. I have my taste buds back...thank you, God! I am finally enjoying water again! I'm eating some ice cream and I am so excited! Food tastes good again!

I can finally sit on a chair, though I try not to do it for long periods of time. I spend many hours on my couch writing on my computer. But I have to stand up and walk around to keep my joints moving so they don't hurt too much.

I enjoy doing the day-to-day *stuff* more than I ever have before. I love going for a walk with William...I love to spend time with my family...I love to see my friends...I love to see people...I love to eat salad and fruit again...I love all food...I really love life!

And...I love Jesus! He has always been my Lord and Savior. My hope is anchored in Him! I want to share the love of Jesus with everyone! I am so grateful for Him!

I love God with all my heart! I know every day that He saved me! I have faith! I always have hope! And, I am truly grateful for Him! I am grateful for this journey with cancer because I appreciate all that I have even more. I want to give God all the glory!

I have learned that life is all about love...because God *is love*. I believe the most important lesson God wants us to learn here is to love God with our whole hearts and to love one another as we love ourselves. Jesus is The Way, The Truth, and The Life! Life on earth is temporal and we will never be fully satisfied here. We were made for more, and God has that "more" planned for us. And, through Jesus we can share a life in eternity with God!

I have never *felt* alone in my journey with cancer. I am grateful to have shared this time in my life with my love, William. He continues to love and support me. One of the qualities I most admire about him is that he always listens. William also loves to take care of me and always provides for our family. I appreciate him and will forever respect him. It's wonderful to share my life with someone I can fully trust. William is a good man and so faithful to me and to our Lord. He loves me, and I love him! Thank you, William! I am eternally grateful!

We are both so grateful to our Lord for blessing us with our children: Courtney, Taylor, Ashley, and Michael. They are our life and truly have wonderful hearts.

They are extremely kind and loving people. They are a blessing to us, and we are proud to be their mom and dad! I want to thank them for loving us always! I love you all!

I am grateful for my parents, Anne and Anton Duswalt, for giving me life. I appreciate their love and support. They have been so caring throughout my life and continue to be daily. I am grateful to them for our daily talks and encouraging words. Thank you for being such beautiful people. I love you dearly.

I am thankful for my brother, Craig, Natasha, Tyler, Ryan and Hayden! I appreciate your love and kindness. Thank you, Craig for your daily calls to check on me. I truly appreciate you! I love you all!

I also want to thank all of my sweet friends! I appreciate your love and support throughout this journey. I will always love and be grateful for you. Thank you for being you!

Going through such a difficult time, I have felt the outpouring of love from so many people. It's nice to share this experience with others. I want to share the love of Christ and bring God all the glory. Through my weakness, I was shown God's strength. I have allowed Him to do wonders in my life. God is good and I can trust Him...and so can you.

God's power is made perfect in weakness. The apostle Paul welcomed this calling to tell about his weakness so he could witness God's power in his life. I was weak and God gave me His strength! He uses our circumstances to mature our character and to make us more like Jesus. Jesus told us we would experience problems here on earth and no one is free from pain or suffering. Cancer definitely brought me closer to God. It is my suffering that drew me closer to God. As Joni Eareckson Tada says, "Only in suffering will we know Jesus."

Now I get to pass on my hope to you. God has a hope, a plan, and a future for my life and for your life. We have heaven waiting for us. We were created by God, for God, and for His purpose.

Jesus says in Revelation 3:20, "Behold, I stand at the door and knock." When will you answer the door?

Made in the USA
Middletown, DE
14 July 2020

12638989R00083